Malcolm X

MALCOLM X
(1925–1965)

# QUOTATIONS
OF
*Malcolm X*

APPLEWOOD BOOKS

For a complete list of books
currently available, please visit us
at www.applewoodbooks.com

ISBN 978-1-4290-9440-5

Manufactured in the USA

# Malcolm X

MALCOLM X was born Malcolm Little on May 19, 1925, in Omaha, Nebraska. He was the fourth of seven children of Louise Helen Little (née Langdon) and Georgia-born Earl Little, an outspoken Baptist lay speaker and a local leader of the Universal Negro Improvement Association (UNIA). Because of troubles with the Ku Klux Klan, the family relocated to Milwaukee, Wisconsin, in 1926 and shortly thereafter to Lansing, Michigan. Malcolm's father died in a streetcar accident in 1932 and his mother was hospitalized because of a "nervous breakdown." Malcolm and his siblings were separated and sent to live in foster homes.

Moving to New York City in 1943, Little lived a turbulent life and became involved in drug dealing, gambling, racketeering, and robbery. The life of crime continued when he moved to Boston, but the law caught up with him in 1946 and he was sentenced to ten years in prison for robbery.

It was while serving time that Little was introduced to the teachings of Elijah Muhammad and the Nation of Islam, a Black nationalist organization. After he was released from prison in 1952, he adopted the name Malcolm X and became the movement's most successful evangelical minister.

Malcolm became a leading and powerful figure in the civil rights movement of the late 1950s and early 1960s. His doctrine of economic self-reliance attracted many followers, while his call for revolution and black independence from white society "by any means necessary" was often viewed as a call to violence.

On March 8, 1964, Malcolm publicly announced his break from the Nation of Islam. He felt that the nation had "gone as far as it can" because of its rigid teachings. He also announced that he was willing to work now with other civil rights leaders like Dr. King.

Also in 1964, Malcolm made a holy pilgrimage to Mecca, Saudi Arabia, the birthplace of the Islamic faith. After his return to the US, he converted to Islam and abandoned his belief in violence and separation of the races.

Some Black Muslims saw Malcom's growing popularity as a challenge to Elijah Muhammad's leadership, and throughout 1964 Malcom received death threats. On February 14, 1965, Malcolm's home was firebombed, but he and his wife and children escaped unharmed. A week later, on February 21, 1965, Malcolm X was assassinated during a speech at the Audubon Ballroom in Manhattan. He was thirty-nine years old and left behind his wife, Betty Shabazz, and four young daughters.

# QUOTATIONS
OF
*Malcolm X*

*T*hese four years of seclusion have proven to be the most enlightening years of my 24 years upon this earth and I feel this 'gift of Time' was Allah's reward to me as His way of saving me from the certain destruction for which I was heading.

—Letter from Norfolk Prison, Massachusetts,
February 15, 1950

*Malcolm X*

*I*slam, the natural religion of Dark Mankind, is sweeping through Black America like a "flaming fire," under the Divine Guidance of Messenger Elijah Muhammad. Fools try to ignore facts, but wise men must face facts to remain wise. Fools refuse to change from their silly ways and beliefs, but the mental flexibility of the wise man permits him to keep an open mind and enables him to readjust himself whenever it becomes necessary for a change.

—Article for the *Los Angeles Herald-Dispatch*, July 18, 1957

*M*essenger Muhammad's teachings have really inspired us with a thirst today for truth. We who follow him are filled with a frenzied craving to wear the Crown of Life, the jewels of which are: Wisdom, Knowledge, Understanding...Freedom, Justice, Equality...Food, Clothing, Shelter... Love, Peace, Happiness. He teaches us that these must be enjoyed while we are living.

—Article for the *Los Angeles Herald-Dispatch*, August 15, 1957

*Malcolm X*

*I*t is true that we have served our Slavemaster willingly for over 300 years without one pay day...and Almighty God Allah has taught Messenger Muhammad that it was our own free labor (sweat and blood) that made it possible for our Slavemaster to be the possessor today of the richest nation on earth.

—Article for the *Los Angeles Herald-Dispatch*, September 5, 1957

*F*reedom is essential to life itself.
Freedom is essential to the development
of the human being. If we don't have
freedom we can never expect justice and
equality. Only after we have freedom do
justice and equality become a reality.

—Harlem Freedom Rally, July 31, 1960

*Malcolm X*

*W*henever you find a man who's in
a position to show power against power
then that man is respected. But you can
take a man who has power and love him
all the rest of your life, nonviolently and
forgivingly and all the rest of those things,
and you won't get anything out of it.

—*New York Amsterdam News*, August 8, 1960

*A*s long as Uncle Sam is against
you, you know you're a good guy.

—Said after meeting Fidel Castro,
September 1960

*Malcolm X*

*O*f all the things that the black man, or any
man for that matter, can study, history is the
best qualified to reward all research. You have
to have a knowledge of history no matter
what you are going to do; anything that you
undertake you have to have a knowledge
of history in order to be successful in it.

—Speech on police brutality,
Los Angeles, California, May 20, 1962

*S*o the religion that we have, the religion of Islam, the religion that makes us Muslims, the religion that The Honorable Elijah Muhammad is teaching us here in America today, is designed to undo in our minds what the white man has done to us. It's designed to undo the type of brainwashing that we have had to undergo for four hundred years at the hands of the white man.

—Speech on police brutality,
Los Angeles, California, May 20, 1962

*Malcolm X*

*C*offee is the only thing I like integrated.

—Comment to Alex Haley, 1963

*Y*ou and I were born at this turning point in history; we are witnessing the fulfillment of prophecy. Our present generation is witnessing the end of colonialism, Europeanism, Westernism, or 'White-ism'...the end of white supremacy, the end of the evil white man's unjust rule.

—Speech before the Nation of Islam, 1963

*Malcolm X*

*T*his is what you should realize. The greatest contribution to this country was that which was contributed by the Black man.

—Call for Reparations apeech, Michigan State University, East Lansing, Michigan, January 23, 1963

*L*incoln said that if he could save
the Union without freeing the slaves,
he would....As for the Emancipation
Proclamation, sir, it was an empty document.
If it freed the slaves, why, a century later,
are we still battling for civil rights?

—Alex Haley interviews Malcolm X, May 1963

*Malcolm X*

*B*rother, do you realize that some of
history's leaders never were recognized
until they were safely in the ground?

—Alex Haley interviews Malcolm X, May 1963

*Malcolm X*

*A* racial explosion is more destructive
than a nuclear explosion.

—Letter to Dr. Martin Luther King Jr., July 31, 1963

*A*merica has a very serious problem. Not only does America have a very serious problem, but our people have a very serious problem. America's problem is us. We're her problem. The only reason she has a problem is she doesn't want us here.

—Statement in Detroit, Michigan, November 10, 1963

*Malcolm X*

*I*f violence is wrong in America, violence is wrong abroad. If it is wrong to be violent defending black women and black children and black babies and black men, then it is wrong for America to draft us and make us violent abroad in defense of her. And if it is right for America to draft us, and teach us how to be violent in defense of her, then it is right for you and me to do whatever is necessary to defend our own people right here in this country.

—Speech at a Northern Negro Grass Roots Leadership Conference, Detroit, Michigan, November 1963

$\mathcal{T}$he race problem can never be solved by listening to this white-minded minority. The white man should try to learn what the Black masses want, and the only way to learn what the Black masses want is by listening to the man who speaks for the Black masses of America.

—God's Judgment of White America (The Chickens Come Home to Roost) speech, December 4, 1963

*Malcolm X*

$\mathcal{R}$evolutions are based upon land. Revolutionaries are the landless against the landlord. Revolutions are never peaceful, never loving, never nonviolent. Nor are they ever compromising. Revolutions are destructive and bloody. Revolutionaries don't compromise with the enemy; they don't even negotiate.

—God's Judgment of White America (The Chickens Come Home to Roost) speech, December 4, 1963

There's nothing in our book, the Quran—
you call it "Ko-ran"—that teaches us to
suffer peacefully. Our religion teaches us
to be intelligent. Be peaceful, be courteous,
obey the law, respect everyone; but if
someone puts his hand on you, send him
to the cemetery. That's a good religion.
In fact, that's that old-time religion.

—Speech in Detroit, Michigan, December 10, 1963

*Malcolm X*

If you stick a knife in my back nine inches
and pull it out six inches, there's no progress.
If you pull it all the way out that's not
progress. Progress is healing the wound that
the blow made. And they haven't even pulled
the knife out much less heal the wound.
They won't even admit the knife is there.

—Television interview, March 1964

*I* will always be a Muslim, teaching what you have taught me, and giving you full credit for what I know and what I am....I am still your brother and servant.

—Letter to Elijah Mohammad, March 11, 1964

*Malcolm X*

*T*here can be no black-white unity until there is first some black unity. There can be no workers' solidarity until there is first some racial solidarity. We cannot think of uniting with others until after we have first united among ourselves. We cannot think of being acceptable to others until we have first proven acceptable to ourselves. One can't unite bananas with scattered leaves.

—"A Declaration of Independence," March 12, 1964

*W*e should be peaceful, law-abiding—
but the time has come for the American
Negro to fight back in self-defense whenever
and wherever he is being unjustly and
unlawfully attacked. If the government
thinks I am wrong for saying this, then
let the government start doing its job.

—"A Declaration of Independence," March 12, 1964

*Malcolm X*

*W*hether we are Christians or Muslims
or nationalists or agnostics or atheists, we
must first learn to forget our differences.
If we have differences, let us differ in the
closet; when we come out in front, let us
not have anything to argue about until
we get finished arguing with the man.

—Speech at Cory Methodist Church,
Cleveland, Ohio, April 3, 1964

We need to expand the civil rights struggle to a higher level—to the level of human rights....Human rights are something you were born with. Human rights are your God-given rights. Human rights are the rights that are recognized by all nations of this earth. And any time anyone violates your human rights, you can take them to the world court.

—Speech at Cory Methodist Church,
Cleveland, Ohio, April 3, 1964

*Malcolm X*

Once you change your philosophy, you change your thought pattern. Once you change your thought pattern, you change your—your attitude. Once you change your attitude, it changes your behavior pattern and then you go on into some action. As long as you gotta sit-down philosophy, you'll have a sit-down thought pattern, and as long as you think that old sit-down thought you'll be in some kind of sit-down action.

—"The Ballot or the Bullet" speech, April 12, 1964

*I*t's time now for you and me to become more politically mature and realize what the ballot is for; what we're supposed to get when we cast a ballot; and that if we don't cast a ballot, it's going to end up in a situation where we're going to have to cast a bullet. It's either a ballot or a bullet.

—"The Ballot or the Bullet" speech, April 12, 1964

*Malcolm X*

*M*y excitement is indescribable. My window faces the sea, westward. The streets are filled with the incoming pilgrims from all over the world, the prayers of Allah and verses from the Quran are on the lips of everyone—never have I seen such a beautiful sight, nor witnessed such a scene, nor felt such an atmosphere.

—Letter from Mecca, Saudi Arabia, April 18, 1964

*I* could see...that perhaps if white Americans could accept the Oneness of God, then perhaps, too, they could accept in reality the Oneness of Man—and cease to measure, and hinder, and harm others in terms of their 'differences' in color.

—Letter from Mecca, Saudi Arabia, April 25, 1964

*Malcolm X*

*I*n the past, yes, I have made sweeping indictments of all white people. I will never be guilty of that again—as I know now that some white people are truly sincere, that some truly are capable of being brotherly toward a Black man. The true Islam has shown me that a blanket indictment of all white people is as wrong as when whites make blanket indictments against Blacks.

—*Village Voice* interview, May 1964

$W$e are African, and we happened to be in America. We're not American. We are people who formerly were Africans who were kidnapped and brought to America. Our forefathers weren't the Pilgrims. We didn't land on Plymouth Rock. The rock was landed on us.

—Speech at founding rally of the Organization of Afro-American Unity, June 28, 1964

*Malcolm X*

$E$ducation is an important element in the struggle for human rights. It is the means to help our children and our people rediscover their identity and thereby increase their self-respect.

—Speech at the founding rally of the Organization of Afro-American Unity, June 28, 1964

The aim of...the Organization of Afro-American Unity is to use whatever means necessary to bring about a society in which the twenty-two million Afro-Americans are recognized and respected as human beings.

—Speech at the founding rally of the Organization of Afro-American Unity, June 28, 1964

*Malcolm X*

We need allies who are going to help us achieve a victory, not allies who are going to tell us to be nonviolent. If a white man wants to be your ally, what does he think of John Brown? You know what John Brown did? He went to war. He was a white man who went to war against white people to help free slaves.... White people call John Brown a nut; they depict him in this image because he was willing to shed blood to free the slaves.

—Speech to the Organization of Afro-American Unity, July 5, 1964

*I* believe in the brotherhood of man, all men, but I don't believe in brotherhood with anybody who doesn't want brotherhood with me. I believe in treating people right, but I'm not going to waste my time trying to treat somebody right who doesn't know how to return the treatment.

—Speech, New York City, December 12, 1964

*Malcolm X*

*V*ictims of racism are created in the image of racists.

—Speech at the Harvard Law School Forum, December 16, 1964

*I*f your present racist agitation against our people there in Alabama causes physical harm to Reverend King or any other Black Americans who are only attempting to enjoy their rights as free human beings,... you and your Ku Klux Klan friends will be met with maximum physical retaliation from those of us who are not handcuffed by the disarming philosophy of nonviolence, and who believe in asserting our right of self-defense—by any means necessary.

—Telegram sent to George Lincoln Rockwell, leader of the American Nazi Party, January 1965

*Malcolm X*

*T*he media's the most powerful entity on earth. They have the power to make the innocent guilty and to make the guilty innocent, and that's power. Because they control the minds of the masses.

—Television interview, 1965

$y$ou can't separate peace from freedom, because no one can be at peace unless he has his freedom.

—Speech in New York City, January 7, 1965

*Malcolm X*

$I$'m for truth, no matter who tells it. I'm for justice, no matter who it is for or against. I'm a human being, first and foremost, and as such I'm for whoever and whatever benefits humanity as a whole.

—Interview for the Pierre Berton Show, Toronto, Ontario, January 19, 1965

$\mathcal{I}$ believe in recognizing every human being as a human being, neither white, Black, brown, nor red. When you are dealing with humanity as one family, there's no question of integration or intermarriage. It's just one human being marrying another human being, or one human being living around and with another human being.

—Interview for the Pierre Berton Show, Toronto, Ontario, January 19, 1965

*Malcolm X*

$\mathcal{I}$ want Dr. [Martin Luther] King to know that I didn't come to Selma to make his job difficult. I really did come thinking I could make it easier. If the white people realize what the alternative is, perhaps they will be more willing to hear Dr. King.

—Conversation with Coretta Scott King, February 1965

*I* was in a house last night that was bombed, my own....It isn't something that made me lose confidence in what I am doing, because my wife understands and I have children...and even in their young age they understand. I think they would rather have a father or brother or whatever the situation may be who will take a stand in the face of any kind of reaction from narrow-minded people...than to compromise and later on have to grow up in shame and in disgrace.

—Speech at the Ford Auditorium in Detroit, February 14, 1965

*E*very time you pick up your newspaper, you see that I'm advocating violence. I have never advocated any violence. I've only said that Black people who are the victims of organized violence perpetrated upon us, we should defend ourselves. I wouldn't call on anybody to be violent without a cause.

—Speech at the Ford Auditorium in Detroit, February 14, 1965

*I*t is a time for martyrs now, and if I am to be one, it will be for the cause of brotherhood. That's the only thing that can save this country.

—Speech in New York City, February 19, 1965

*Malcolm X*

*T*o me the earth's most explosive and pernicious evil is racism, the inability of God's creatures to live as One, especially in the Western world.

—*The Autobiography of Malcolm X* (1965)

*My* alma mater was books, a good library. Every time I catch a plane, I have with me a book that I want to read—and that's a lot of books these days. If I weren't out here every day battling the white man, I could spend the rest of my life reading, just satisfying my curiosity—because you can hardly mention anything I'm not curious about.

—*The Autobiography of Malcolm X* (1965)

*Malcolm X*

One day, may we all meet together in the light of understanding.

—*The Autobiography of Malcolm X* (1965)

*Malcolm X*

*If* you aren't careful, the newspapers will have you hating the people who are being oppressed and loving the people who are doing the oppressing.

—*The Autobiography of Malcolm X* (1965)

*A*nd if I can die having brought any light, having exposed any meaningful truth that will help to destroy the racist cancer that is malignant in the body of America—then, all of the credit is due to Allah. Only the mistakes have been mine.

–*The Autobiography of Malcolm X* (1965)

*P*ower in defense of freedom is greater than power in behalf of tyranny and oppression.

–*Malcolm X Speaks* (1965)

*N*obody can give you freedom. Nobody can give you equality or justice or anything. If you're a man, you take it.

–*Malcolm X Speaks* (1965)

*I* believe in a religion that believes in freedom. Any time I have to accept a religion that won't let me fight a battle for my people, I say to hell with that religion.

—*By Any Means Necessary* (1970)

*Malcolm X*

*I* for one will join with anyone—I don't care what color you are—as long as you want to change the miserable condition that exists on this earth.

—*By Any Means Necessary* (1970)

Malcolm X